Ready

MW01281965

What to Know Before You Go

Krystal Waterz

SECOND EDITION

PUBLISHED BY:
Orlando Home Solutions, LLC

Copyright © 2013
All rights reserved.

Be sure to check out my other travel books!

Introduction

Bon Voyage!

Introduction

Cruising is an investment. Not only is it a monetary investment, it's an investment of your precious time. A time to recharge your batteries, spend quality time with your family and friends or just relax ….. read a good book, gaze out at the ocean, watch the sun set, take in a great show or savor a gourmet dinner. Cruising can – and should – be one of the best vacations you ever take. My book will help you sort out some of the decision-making a cruise takes. What kind of cruise am I looking for? Is picking a cabin really important and why? What's included in my cruise? How can I save money? Whether this is your first cruise or your 15th cruise, the tips in my book can help you plan the best vacation ever!

I took my first cruise over 20 years ago and after that first seven day cruise, I was hooked! I loved being able to unpack once and at the same time, travel to some really fun and interesting locations. Onboard, I could participate in a variety of activities all day long or just sit out on the deck or balcony and read a book or take nap. I could do as much – or as little as I wanted. Most of my expenses were paid up front. Meals, entertainment and my room were already covered - before I ever stepped onboard! It took the worries out of where I went and how I got there. I was pampered, spoiled and couldn't wait to go again.

Paradise Point, St. Thomas USVI

Over the years, by my own trial and errors, I discovered some things I WISH I had known before I ever started cruising. I hope the following tips will help you plan one of the best vacations you will ever take!

Chapter 1. Choosing a Ship & Getting the Most Bang for your Buck

There are so many cruise lines to choose from so the first thing you need to decide is what type of cruise suits you. I've cruised on several of the more popular lines so here's my own **personal opinion** on those lines.

Carnival Cruise Lines. Carnival is the #1 cruise line in the world. It was on Carnival Holiday that I took my very first cruise back in 1990. This cruise line gets the reputation of being a party ship. I've cruised on Carnival more than any other cruise line (to date) and it used to be my favorite but it no longer holds that title for me. You can get some great deals on Carnival but some of the other major lines have very competitive prices so I think pricing depends more on time of year, where you're going, how long your cruise will be and several other factors. Carnival has lots of fun activities. The food is just as good (and sometimes better) as the other major lines. I don't think it's just a party ship. A lot of families cruise Carnival and I personally feel they have a good children's program. My daughter went to Camp Carnival several times when she was younger and had a blast!

The shorter cruises - 3, 4 or 5 days tend to attract a younger crowd. If you cruise over Spring Break, chances are you'll also get the younger college crowd - and it will probably feel like a party ship.

Carnival's ships are – well - bright and colorful. Some say gaudy and tacky. They don't bother me. This is a vacation, not my home so if I'm not 100% in love with the décor, it's not a big deal. In a few days I won't have to see it again. If anything, it reminds me I'm on vacation and that makes me happy.

Their food is comparable to other cruise lines. I have some definite favorites like their Chocolate Melting Cake or pressed Turkey Ruben from their deli. The Mongolian Wok is very popular and worth the wait. Food is subjective. You will always find good and bad whether you're dining on a cruise ship or in a land-based restaurant. Carnival offers a good variety. The larger, newer ships offer a couple specialty restaurants (that will cost extra). Included in your cruise are other options such as the deli, a pizza / pasta station and if you're lucky, a taste bar with some savory little samples, Guy Fieri's burgers and more.

Celebrity Cruise Lines. I have been on one Celebrity cruise so my experience is based on one ship. I wanted to try Celebrity because it's touted as a more "upscale" luxurious cruise. The décor is elegant, the food is superior, the entertainment a step above other cruise lines. I didn't find any of that. I thought all of the above was comparable to other cruise lines - and not worth paying more.

Two things that did stand out to me is the majority of passengers were retirement age/beyond and entertainment was geared towards this crowd. Even the music – live and otherwise – was a little dated to me. If you're looking for a more laid-back, low-key cruise, this would probably be a good choice.

The other thing I noticed about Celebrity - and this is definitely a positive – the shower in our cabin bathroom was the largest I've ever had on a cruise ship! I could actually turn around in the shower without touching the wall or end up having the shower curtain stuck to my body! It was awesome.

Norwegian Cruise Line. My first cruise on Norwegian was in Hawaii. We spent 7 days cruising around the Hawaiian Islands and it was wonderful. I wouldn't hesitate to recommend a Hawaiian cruise. I could write a whole book on that trip alone.

I have been on a few NCL cruises since that first one and there are several things I like about this line. The ships are quite nice. They use a lot of wood and glass in their interior designs. It has good flow for getting around. Entertainment is pretty similar to other cruise lines. I like their Freestyle Dining = no set dining time. I think it works well because the wait staff doesn't have to juggle both open dining and set dining times like several other cruise lines do. One of my favorite eating places on Norwegian is the Longboard Bar. I'm not sure if all ships offer this, but the cruises I have been on they did. This bar / restaurant reminds me of the burger joint down the street. They're open later in the evening and although the menu is somewhat limited, it does include burgers, fries and my favorite – chicken wings! I'm sure I'll cruise on Norwegian again and again. They offer a great product and prices are competitive to other mass lines.

Royal Caribbean. Last but not least is Royal Caribbean. They are my favorite but they weren't always. My first Royal Caribbean cruise was on Mariner of the Seas. This was the most expensive cruise my husband and I ever booked and I was deeply disappointed. We had a problem in the dining room and another with our cabin. Neither issue was addressed or resolved. It did not live up to what I had envisioned and after that cruise, I vowed never to cruise them again.

Fast forward a few years and a great deal came up on one of their older ships, close to home so my husband and I said, "What the heck. We'll try it again." We had a great cruise. Loved the ship, loved the food and everything else about it. The experience was the complete opposite of our first Royal Caribbean cruise.

Since then, we've cruised this line several times and have never again been disappointed.

So what makes Royal Caribbean my personal favorite? Well, I'm glad you asked! It would be hard to pinpoint a number one thing but it could possibly be the ships themselves. The activities are more unique and interesting. Many of their ships offer rock wall climbing, ice skating, the FlowRider, the promenade for parades and other activities. I love the Viking Lounge which has amazing

Royal Caribbean – Liberty of the Seas

views of not only the ocean but the pool deck and all the activities going on – minus the crowds and noise. For the most part, it's a nice, peaceful place to read or just relax on a sea day. The shows can be good to very good. I like the ice show – very entertaining. The food is comparable to the other lines but I give Royal the edge on dining rooms themselves. They just seem a little nicer.

Last but not least, I think the member benefits are far superior to Carnival. We're Platinum on Carnival and Gold on Royal Caribbean. Platinum being a higher status with more cruises under our belt should give us some nice benefits but they're lacking.

Gold on Royal Caribbean (with less cruises than we've taken on Carnival) gives us about the same benefits. The more cruises on Royal, the better the perks. This may not matter to a lot of people but if you cruise a lot (or plan on a lot of future cruises) and they have a recognition program for repeat guests, it should have value.

One more thing to consider when choosing a cruise line and particular ship is what activities do they offer? If you have children, teenagers or any young adults that will be vacationing with you, I can almost guarantee they will LOVE Royal Caribbean's newer ships. Our last cruise on Royal Caribbean was on Liberty of the Seas. They had rock wall climbing, an ice skating rink, FlowRider. Heck, they even had a boxing ring! The kids on board were having a great time! Even the kiddie pool area was impressive.

Royal Caribbean – Liberty of the Seas

Royal Caribbean – Liberty of the Seas. Rock Wall Climbing

Most of the older cruise ships offer a children's water park, mini golf, basketball court, a variety of activities based on age and more. But for all the bells and whistles, you'll have to choose newer ships or ones that have been updated.

Royal Caribbean – Liberty of the Seas

With that in mind, if you're not bringing children or young adults with you and you're looking for a more relaxing vacation with few children on board, you might just want to avoid the ships I just described. Liberty of the Seas was full of kids which was a little surprising since it was mid-April and we didn't think they were out of school for summer break yet.

All of these ships have comparable prices, depending on a lot of different factors. If price is your #1 consideration, I would look at all of the above cruise lines and any others that might be a good fit, since they should be in the same ballpark price-wise with Celebrity more than likely at the top end.

If you'd like to get a little more info and look at pictures of all the different ships, check out beyondships.com.

Now on to getting the best price possible on your cruise!

Timing or more accurately - time of year you plan to cruise

10

- is everything. Cruise prices change daily, depending on a lot of different factors. The closer the ship gets to filling up, the higher the price of the cabin. Sometimes you get the best deal by booking well in advance and you may be able to get a price guarantee when you book. If the price drops before you sail, you get that better price!

You can also get a good price is you're flexible and can book on very short notice. We've gotten some of the best deals ever when we booked last minute. The first one in April of last year, we booked on Friday and sailed on Monday. Last September, we booked on a Wednesday and sailed on Monday. Since we have flexibility to cruise short notice, we had been keeping an eye on prices and when they dropped significantly, we booked.

The downside to booking last minute is you're limited on what cabins are still available. The cruise in April was guaranteed stateroom in an inside cabin. Admittedly, I was nervous as I had never booked a guaranteed room before. We got lucky and got a really great room! It was one floor below the Lido deck. Now normally, this might not be an ideal location (think scraping lounge chairs, late night parties) but we just happened to be directly under the Spa - so it was nice and quiet. Below us was a floor of cabins. And it was quiet. Only one flight of stairs and we were on Lido.

One of our recent cruises was the cheapest we ever paid. It was four nights for $375 for both of us – including taxes and port charges. We prepaid our tips and it came in at just under $500 ($475). I was able to pick the cabin on Deck 2, center ship. The room was nice and quiet but unfortunately the toilet in our cabin worked about 40% of the time. There's nothing worse than pushing the button after you're done and – nothing happens!

The first two times we complained, guest services told us someone had flushed something down the toilet that clogged it. The room steward told us a completely different story. Maintenance tried to fix the problem numerous times but to no avail. (And to those of you concerned that – horrors! – maintenance will have to come in to your bathroom – that you JUST used, then I'm here to make you feel a whole lot better. They do not. There's an access panel in the hallway, just outside your door. They tinker around in there doing mysterious stuff and VOILA – it starts working again!) OK, back to my story!

After day two of our toilet issue, they moved us to a different room, up one floor and wayyyyy down the hall. It was a similar room (nope, no upgrade for our "inconvenience"). I was pretty happy to have a flushing toilet (ahh, the little things in life) but it did put a damper on our mood as we had to pack and unpack twice. Had I had more time to research this ship, I would have discovered that this ship was "stretched" a few years ago – a section was added to the center of the ship which included the area our cabin was in. My theory is when they added to this ship, the vacuum system for the toilets in this section got messed up. We discovered several other cabins close to ours had the same issue.

Another good time to find bargain prices for a particular sailing is 60 – 90 (and some up to 120) days prior to departure. This is because it's the cut off for existing travelers to cancel their booked cruise without penalty. Once the deadline passes and cruisers are no longer able to cancel without losing their deposit (or more, depending on how much they've forked over), the cruise lines know exactly how many cabins they need fill and if they have too many left open, they'll start reducing fares to sell out the ship.

One major consideration is the time of year you want to cruise. Generally, the cheapest time of year to cruise is during hurricane season. Having said that, summer months tend to be more expensive since school-age children are off for the summer and that's when families will go - so ships fill up quickly. Some of the best prices could be late September, the Month of October into early November when kids are back in school (and it's still considered Hurricane Season).

I've cruised several times during hurricane season and for the most part, been pretty lucky. One of our more recent cruises was in early September and a small (Category 1) hurricane had just gone through the Bahamas only a couple days before we left. I spent a week worrying about this storm. Would it stall and sit over the Bahamas? Would it become stronger and last longer than predicted? By the time my ship set sail, the storm was gone and it was one of the smoothest sailings ever.

Centrum - Looking up at Glass Elevators – Royal Caribbean

On the other hand, I took a cruise out of Miami in late October, about a week after a larger category hurricane had passed through. I thought by the time we sailed the seas would be fairly calm and yet the first couple days, it was very rough and a lot of people suffered from motion sickness.

You can never predict the weather during hurricane season so be prepared to possibly endure some rough seas, bad weather and itinerary changes the cruise line may make to avoid the storm if you decide to cruise during this time of year.

Another good time to cruise is early December. Hurricane season is over. Outside temperatures are still very nice in the Bahamas and Caribbean and it's just not a high demand time of year. I've seen some of the best deals the first week of December.

Peak season with highest prices are obviously the holidays – Spring Break, Christmas through New Year's or anytime during the summer when families vacation with children all tend to have higher rates.

If you're feeling adventurous and have lots of time, repositioning or transatlantic cruises can be a great deal. The upside – or the downside, depending on how you look at it, will be the amount of time you'll be on the ship. I wouldn't recommend this for a first-time cruiser only because you may find out you hate cruising and then you're stuck on that ship for a lot longer than you want to be.

So you finally found the perfect cruise. A great price, ports you've been dying to visit, vacation time you've been approved for – but what about the cabin? Maybe you're thinking – who cares? It's just a room, right? I don't plan on spending that much time in it anyways… Maybe you're right but for at least half the people reading this book – cabin location will be important. Let me explain why.

Rule of thumb: In most cases, the more desirable the cabin (balcony vs. ocean view vs. inside), the higher the price. It's the same thing if you booked a hotel room. A balcony room, facing the ocean will be more expensive than a window facing the parking lot, right?

I recommend comparing rates by using some of the major

online search engines such as Expedia, Cruisesonly.com, etc. That will give you a good snapshot of what's available on the various lines and at what price. Check the actual cruise line, as well to see if you can get a better rate. I've found the prices to be similar but sometimes on-line booking sites throw in an extra perk such as a free room upgrade, onboard credit or free soda card.

Before you book your cruise and are locked in, make sure you know what the port charges and taxes will be. If booking online, this amount will show up on the screen before you hit the payment button. Port charges and taxes will vary depending on where you go and for how long. I looked at a cruise out of Miami a few months ago. It was a great price and I was pretty excited – until I got to the end when I found out the port charges and taxes were more than the cruise!!!!

One of the best things out there I see being offered more and more these days is 24 hour courtesy holds (mainly on the specific cruise line's website). No too long ago, there was no such thing as hold your room for 24 hours. It was buy and pay or lose that rate. If thcy offer a 24 hour-hold – TAKE IT! You have nothing to lose! That'll give you a chance to check with Grandma to see if she'll watch the kids while you're gone, check airline rates (what if airfare will cost more than the cruise? Not such a great bargain anymore) and last but not least – maybe you can find a better rate or a freebie another website may be offering

To use a travel agent or not to use a travel agent? This is a personal preference. I've done both. My first few cruises were through a travel agent and although they were perfectly fine, as time went on I felt I knew enough – and many times more - about cruising than the agent. I could get exactly what I wanted on my own. If you had the right travel agent, could you get a better price or advice that's helpful and will save you some headaches? Yeah, I'm sure you could. Again, it's a personal preference. If you do decide to use a travel agent, pick someone who specializes in cruises and who has been on several of their own.

Once more note on picking your cruise. There are a lot of "theme cruises" out there that vary from "Alternative Lifestyle" group cruises to "Food and Wine" group cruises. If you want to check out who might be on your cruise before you book, take a look at "themecruisefinder.com."

Carnival Freedom – St. Thomas, USVI

Chapter 2. Location, Location, Location

Cabin location is important! Before you secure your cabin with a deposit (sometimes non-refundable, depending on how close to the departure date you are), make sure you check out your cabin location! To some, this may not be a big deal but if you are a light sleeper or prone to motion sickness, this can mean the difference between an awesome cruise - or vacation nightmare.

For instance, if you tend to get motion sickness, you do not want your cabin in the front of the ship. There's a lot of motion in the front and if the seas are rough, it will be even worse. The best location for those prone to motion is the center of the ship in a lower deck cabin.

QUICK TIP: Looking to find out what sea conditions you might encounter? Check out http://www.stormsurf.com and click on QuikCAST tab!

If you're a light sleeper, certain cabins in the front can be very noisy – especially when the ship docks in port. If you are in one of those "lucky" cabins, when they drop the anchor it will wake you out of a sound sleep. Trust me. This is coming from the voice of experience!

The best possible room (in my opinion) is one that has an entire floor of cabins above and below it.   My husband & I once made the mistake of picking a cabin that was directly above the main lounge. Every time the orchestra practiced (not to mention during the shows), the floor vibrated. It was extremely loud. If they no longer have live orchestra onboard, it may be a non-issue.

Bronze Statue – Enchantment of the Seas, Royal Caribbean

When you're looking at the ship layout, be sure to note any mysterious "empty" spaces beside or behind your room. Cruise ships use every inch of space on board. These blank areas could be service elevators or storage rooms for room steward supplies and where they store their carts. We had a cabin like that once. Very early every morning, the room stewards pulled their carts from the "secret closet" and in the process banged into the walls adjoining our room. We complained to guest services and not only did the noise stop, we got a $50 onboard credit each for our "inconvenience." We didn't ask for it but it was a nice gesture.

If you book a cabin with a balcony, be aware that balconies on certain cruise lines have sliding doors while others are hinged and can easily slam shut. We've had balconies with both and the sliding doors are so much nicer! Some cruise lines no longer allow smoking on private balconies but others still do (Carnival). Balconies are popular with smokers so if you're a non-smoker, make sure you will be OK with potentially being next to a cabin with a smoker.

Chapter 3. Cabin Quick Guide

Cabins range from small inside to larger suites. The inside cabins tend to be the cheapest rooms onboard. Next in price would be ocean view cabins. Still cheaper than balconies or suites, they're a little more money than inside cabins and usually a little roomier. If you book an ocean view cabin, make sure you will actually have a view. Some have "obstructed views" and chances are, you'll be looking at the side of a lifeboat or the ship's metal framework.

Balconies are nice. I love balconies but again, check the location. There are good balconies and not-so-good. I've never booked a suite but plan on it someday. Tip charges are higher in suites but there are also more amenities.

For two people, even the smallest cabin will normally be just fine. You should have plenty of closet and storage space but not a lot of room to walk around. (Tip: put your empty suitcases under the bed.) The bathrooms are small and the showers are even smaller. Visualize a small shower. Got it? OK, cut that in half and that's the size shower you'll have. And no, I'm not kidding.

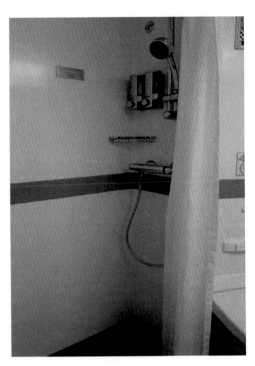

Carnival Freedom – Cabin Shower

I don't have a good tip for managing to shower in these little areas other than possibly leaving the shower door/curtain open for more room. (On a side note, I'm not sure if I have a really sensitive nose but at least half the cruises I've been on, I ask the cabin steward to replace the shower curtain because it has a bad odor and leaves the bathroom smelling not so nice.)

We just got back from a 7 day cruise and after checking out the bathroom I thought, "Nice. No bad shower curtain smell!" The next morning my husband came out of the bathroom and asked me if I noticed the blood stains on the shower curtain. Sheesh! I guess yucky shower curtains are the norm for me!

Inside Cabin – Royal Caribbean Cruise Line

One last shower tip. If you really can't use your shower, the bathrooms near the spa/gym have large, private showers that anyone can use – not just people paying for spa treatments. They are way larger than the one in your cabin.

Carnival Freedom – Spa Shower

Years ago, certain cruise lines would leave a nice little goody pack in the bath which included toothpaste, mouth wash, shaving cream, razors, etc. With all of the cutbacks, expect liquid soap and possibly shampoo in a wall dispenser located in the shower. Plan on bringing all other toiletries with you. They may have more available in suites but check with the cruise line before packing.

Cabin Bathroom – Carnival Dream

Carnival Dream – Balcony Cabin

The closet should have hangers. If you need more hangers, don't be afraid to ask! Certain cruise lines still provide bathrobes to use while onboard and towels to take onshore or in port while others no longer have them.

Some cabins have small refrigerators and others (some of the older ships) do not. If you have a cabin with a refrigerator, you'll find it full of sodas and goodies to purchase at a hefty price. You can ask the room steward to remove these items for the duration of your cruise and then put your own stuff inside.

There's typically a really large bottle of water on the counter you can purchase for several bucks. This is really getting off track but I thought I'd share this story. We cruised with friends recently and one morning, one of them decided to drink the big

26

bottle of water on the counter (btw, they'll just tack the cost onto your account if you drink it and then the room steward will replace it with another – just in case you want more). Anyways, she went to take the lid off and the seal was already broken. So, someone drank the water, replaced it with some other kind of water – probably out of the bathroom sink – and then put the lid back on – just so they wouldn't have to pay for it!

Chapter 4. Packing for your cruise

What not to forget. One of my favorite sayings is, "Bring twice as much money and half the clothes." I always come back after a cruise with a pile of clothes I never wore. Here are a few things you don't want to forget. (These are not in any particular order.)

Carry-On Bag. I put this at the front of the packing list for a very important reason! What you pack in your carry-on bag could make the difference between a miserable vacation and great vacation!

If the cruise line loses your luggage, they will give you a small toiletry bag with toothbrush, toothpaste, mouthwash, comb, a bar of soap and disposable razor. None of these items are brand name or high quality but could get you through a night, if absolutely necessary.

Some cruise lines require any beverages you bring on board – be carried on (water, soda, allowed alcohol.) Others will let you to put beverages in your checked bags. Each line is different so be sure to check your cruise line's policy.

My next suggestion is based on personal experience. Carry on one complete change of clothing for each person and any medication, contact lenses, solutions, and all valuables. When packing, ask yourself, if the cruise line loses my luggage (even if only for one night), what do I need to have with me that can't be replaced or I can't live without?

Toss in some swimwear and sunscreen. You'll be able to use the pool as soon as you board but won't have your luggage delivered to your stateroom until later in the day.

Passport. I strongly recommend a passport. U.S. Homeland Security and the cruise lines will allow U.S. citizens to board with photo ID and original birth certificate if the cruise originates in the U.S. and is a closed-loop cruise. (Meaning the ship departs from a U.S. port and returns to a U.S. port.) The birth certificate must be an original, issued by the local government in the area in which you were born (i.e., the county) with the raised seal. It cannot be a copy and it cannot be a hospital record of birth provided by the hospital.

The reason I strongly recommend bringing a passport versus the photo ID and birth certificate is - if something happens when you're on your vacation – like an emergency - where you don't return from your trip via that cruise ship, you may have a difficult time getting back into the U.S. If you become ill and need to leave your cruise mid-trip and return to the U.S. or you miss your ship and have to fly back to the U.S. are examples of when you would absolutely want to have a passport.

Some cruise lines require that your passport be valid up to 6 months after your cruise ends. For example, if you return from your cruise on December 31st, your passport may have to be valid through June 30th of the following year.

Power Strip or Extension Cord. Some cabins have only one or two outlets. One is in the bathroom and one or two are typically located in the desk area. If you bring a laptop and a couple cell phones, you won't have enough outlets. I've heard that some cruise lines don't allow power strips or extension cords but I've brought them on almost every cruise and after 25 cruises, never had a problem.

Flashlight. This may seem like an odd item to pack but if the ship were to lose power and the only light you have is the emergency light outside your cabin, that flashlight will come in handy.

Binoculars. These would be especially useful if you are going to say, Alaska and there is a lot to see right from the balcony.

Beverages. We covered this in an earlier tip but it doesn't hurt to say it again. This will definitely save you money. Some cruise lines carry only Pepsi products while others only Coke. Check with the cruise line to see what brand they carry if the brand of soda you drink is important to you. Plus, bringing your own with you will save some $$.

Tennis shoes or Closed-toe Shoes. A lot of excursions require these shoes. No flip flops or sandals allowed. Plus, if you plan on doing a lot of walking, tennis shoes will be more comfortable and less chance of getting blisters.

Extra Batteries. You can buy them on board if you forget but they are expensive!

Toothbrush Holder. This may seem a little odd, but I just don't like setting my toothbrush on the counter or inside one of the glasses they leave in the bathroom.

Sunglasses and Sunscreen. Now you may be saying, "How could I possibly forget these?" If you're coming from the frozen tundra up North (for me it was Michigan), in the middle of winter, the last thing you're thinking about is sunscreen and sunglasses.

Walkie-Talkies. If you have children that may be in the kid's camp or allowed some freedom aboard the ship, these will be pretty useful to keep track of them.

Dress Clothes. If you plan on dining in the main dining room during one of the formal nights, you will want to bring something nice to wear. Dress slacks and a button down or collared shirt for men and dress slacks and nice blouse for women will suffice. Of course, you can go all out and wear suits, tuxes and formal gowns. I like to dress up for formal night and get several pictures taken by the photographers.

Most of the time, we don't buy the pictures since we already have quite a few but occasionally we'll buy one. One of our favorites – hanging proudly on my dining room wall - is a formal picture we had taken with all three of our children. It was worth every penny!

Snorkeling Gear (if applicable). If you plan on snorkeling, I suggest bringing your own snorkeling equipment. The first time I ever went snorkeling was in Saint Croix. It was a ship excursion and I used their snorkeling equipment. It was a great excursion – a day at the beach and I got to see some very exotic sea life. A couple days later, I became deathly ill and to this day I believe the snorkeling gear was not sanitized and that is what made me sick. For less than $20 you can buy your own and know that what you are using is clean. Some cruise lines also sell sets. Not sure what they charge, though.

Water Shoes. If you plan on snorkeling or doing a beach day, water shoes would come in very handy. Some of the beaches have sharp rocks close to shore.

Bug Repellant. You may or may not need this, depending on excursions. We once went cave tubing in a Belize rainforest and I didn't think to bring bug spray with me. It sure would have saved me a few bug bites!

Over the Door Shoe Organizer. This can be used not only to put your shoes in but as storage for other items you want to keep track of. (If you decided to bring an organizer, make sure it won't damage the cabin door. Some lines no longer allow you to use them.)

Hand Sanitizer. Small bottle of hand sanitizer or wet wipes.

Highlighter. Each day you'll get a flyer that lists the ship activities for that day. You can use your highlighter to mark what activities you don't want to miss.

Alarm Clock. The majority of cabins do not have clocks or alarm clocks. Battery is best. Remember the limited number of outlets? And if you do have an extra outlet, chances are it's not near your bed!

Hair Dryer (maybe). Some cabins have hair dryers and others do not. Check with the cruise line before you go.

Air Freshener. For the bathroom. Most bathrooms don't have fans or even decent ventilation.

Jacket or Sweater. Some areas of the ship are cold so bring a jacket or sweater - just in case.

Extra, Empty Bag or Suitcase. If you plan on buying a lot of trinkets, souvenirs, clothes or alcohol, you might want to bring an extra bag or suitcase to bring your goodies home. If you plan on bringing drinks onboard such as bottled water or sodas, you may have enough space once you empty out the drinks to pack your extras in that luggage space. If you're flying in and out for your cruise, just remember the extra baggage charge you will pay for your purchases.

Watch. Bring a watch, set it to the ship's time and don't change it. In port, you'll need to keep track of the time you need to be back on the ship. Some ports may be in a different time zone so again, **be sure your watch is set to the ship's time.** Some may think, "Well, I don't need a watch, I can check my cell phone." This will work fine if you're able to use your cell phone. I talk about this later in the book but it never hurts to mention it twice. Some cell phone providers charge exorbitant roaming fees and if you can't switch to "airplane mode" or another non-roaming option, you may be better off keeping your phone turned off for the duration of your cruise. (And isn't that what a vacation is about anyways – getting away from it all? Unless, of course, you have small children at home. Then you're excused from this lecture!) This is when a wrist watch or other watch will be very useful.

Water Bottle Filter. Skip the case of bottled water! Instead, pack a water bottle filter. Some of these can be used for months before the small, charcoal filter has to be replaced.

Sadly, I didn't come up with this idea myself. Our friends cruised with us recently and while we were lugging heavy cases of water onboard, they had two sport-size bottles in their backpack that took up little space and weighed next to nothing!

Waterproof Case. If you plan on snorkeling or swimming and won't have a locker available to use or someone to constantly be watching your belongings, I recommend a waterproof case to hold your money, passports, room cards, anything of value. For extra insurance, put in a Ziploc bag first and then place inside the waterproof case.

Photocopies of Important Documents. Make a copy of your passport, return airline tickets, driver's license, credit cards, etc. and keep that copy in your luggage or room safe. Or take a picture of it so you'll have a copy on your phone!

$1 Bills and $5 Bills. Bring some $1 bills and $5 bills to tip porters, for room service delivery, excursion tour guides, etc.

Ear Plugs. If you're a light sleeper, ear plugs might come in handy. The hallways in front of your cabin can get very noisy at night with other passengers who don't realize it's 3:00 o'clock in the morning and others might be trying to sleep!

Another option is a white noise machine. We finally invested in one about a year ago and take it not only on cruises but anywhere we travel. They're awesome and not terribly expensive.

Night Light. The cabins are very dark when the lights are turned off and curtains drawn. This will be useful if you need to make a trip to the bathroom in the middle of the night.

Motion Sickness Medicine. If you're prone to motion sickness, you may need this. They sell it in the shops on board but is a lot cheaper if you purchase beforehand. If you don't like medication or you have children who are prone to motion sickness and don't like the idea of giving them seasick pills, you can try the Sea Bands (wrist bands for motion sickness). Most drugstores and pharmacies carry these. They're also nice because they're re-usable.

Small First-aid Kit that Includes Band-Aids. Aspirin, Ibuprofen, medicine for upset tummies. I'm not sure how I manage to do this, but I always end up with blisters on every single cruise - even when wearing my "every day" shoes!

Dollar Store Ponchos. I wish I listened to my own advice on this one. We have half dozen at home but forgot to bring them on one of our last cruises. It rained our entire walk/jog from the cruise ship into Nassau welcome center. We were docked at the very last slip. The one on the very end. And if you've ever cruised to Nassau, you're laughing at me right now. That's not nice! And if you haven't cruised to Nassau before – just bring a rain poncho or an umbrella.

Bright Cloth or Bow to Tie on Your Luggage. It will be easier to identify at the airport and after your cruise. Also, don't put your entire address on the luggage tag for safety reasons. A name and cabin number is sufficient.

Socks and Long Pants. I only add this because, if you're going on a Royal Caribbean cruise – or another line that has an ice rink and they have open skate, you'll need to have a pair of long pants and socks to be allowed on the ice.

Chapter 5. Getting to the Port (Driving)

Parking at the port can be expensive. Each port charges a different per day price. It's fairly easy to find off-site parking lots that are very close to the port but cost a whole lot less than parking at the port. It won't be as convenient since you'll have to take a shuttle from the parking lot to the port and then shuttle back to your vehicle when the cruise is over but if you are taking a longer cruise, this could definitely save you some $$.

If you plan on driving and spending the night before or after the sailing at a local hotel, many area hotels offer free parking if you book just one night's stay. Internet search will give you some area hotels near the port that offer this free parking program.

Dames Point Bridge, Jacksonville, FL
(Only Inches To Clear Bridge! Yikes!)

If you do decide to stay and use the parking program, I suggest booking early. Make sure you let the hotel know that you plan on leaving your vehicle in their parking lot during your cruise. When you check into the hotel, **remind** the front desk you are leaving your vehicle for the duration of your cruise and that you'll need to reserve a spot on the shuttle the next morning to take you to the cruise port. Be sure to confirm the time the shuttle will be leaving the hotel and be there a few minutes early! We've seen

Port Everglades, Ft. Lauderdale, FL

people who didn't bother reminding the hotel and when they tried to catch the shuttle in the morning, there wasn't any room for them. This is not a good way to start a nice relaxing vacation.

The majority of the hotels (particularly those out of Miami and Ft. Lauderdale) only offer free shuttle **TO** the port. After the cruise is over, you'll need to take a taxi back to the hotel to retrieve your vehicle. Remember to grab a business card from the hotel before you hop on the shuttle. It's amazing what a week's vacation and relaxation will do to your brain.

Our last cruise out of Miami, I remembered to grab their business card with the hotel's address and it's a good thing. I remembered the name of the hotel but couldn't for the life of me remember exactly what street it was on.

Royal Promenade, Royal Caribbean – Liberty of the Seas

Chapter 6. Cash and Credit Card Use

Be sure to contact your credit card company before you leave home. Some credit card companies will put a hold on your card if they think there's suspicious activity (charges in a foreign country). Also keep in mind, the cruise line will put a specific dollar amount on hold on your card until your trip is complete.

You can get cash on **some** ships without using the ship's expensive ATM's. Go to the casino & sign up for their player's club card. (This definitely won't work on Disney ships – they don't have casinos.) Sit down at a slot machine where you can transfer money from your onboard charge account to your player's club card. After the money has been transferred, take the card to the cashier and tell them you want to cash out your card. BEWARE, they will only allow you to do this once or twice before they catch on and no longer allow you to cash out.

Chapter 7. On Board Charge Account

One of the first things you do prior to boarding the ship is set up the on board charge account. You'll need a charge card or pay cash up front. The only time you'll use cash on board is in the casino or for tipping room service. You'll use your room card for all onboard store purchases, buying alcoholic drinks or soda (unless you buy the beverage packages). If you purchase a shore excursion from the cruise line, this will be added to your onboard account. Specialty restaurants and spa services are also charged to your onboard account.

Tipping your tour guide after an excursion will be at your discretion and in cash.

If one of your stops is a cruise line's private island, you'll use your cruise ship card for beverage purchases on the island. Yes! They bring those nice, big, tropical beverages on shore! If you purchase any trinkets or gifts from the vendors on the private islands, you may need to pay for the purchase in cash.

If you don't prepay your gratuities, most cruise lines will automatically add the gratuities at some point during your cruise.

On some of the newer cruise ships, you can check your onboard account balance on your room cabin's television. I recommend checking at least a day before your cruise ends so you can settle any discrepancies. The last night of the cruise, later in the day, guest services gets very busy with passengers who have issues with their onboard accounts.

Some cruise lines will leave a copy of your onboard charges either under your cabin door or near the outside of your door in the early morning of your departure day. You can get a printout of onboard charges at one of the kiosks or if your cruise ship doesn't have a kiosk, ask for a copy at guest services.

Chapter 8. Booking the Best Excursions

Some cruisers want to see and do everything while others feel the ship is the destination and are not at all interested in what they can see and do in port. If you're feeling adventurous and want to see what the port has to offer, I have a couple suggestions.

Typically, booking an excursion through the cruise line will be more expensive than booking an independent tour on your own - and choices are limited.

If you booked an excursion on line prior to cruising, you may want to double check to make sure they have your reservation in their system. I've heard of people who booked on-line only to find out the ship had no record of the reservation when they got there.

Disclaimer Alert! This is only my personal opinion on booking excursions through the cruise line vs. on your own. This is a hot topic and everyone has their own opinion! If you have a full day in port – say eight or more hours – and you're looking at taking a four hour or less excursion that departs as soon as you arrive in port, you can be pretty confident you'll make it back to the ship in plenty of time before it sets sail.

If you find an excursion through an independent company that is a lot cheaper than a similar ship excursion, it will be worthwhile to investigate further. Do the research and make sure you're dealing with a reputable company. On-line reviews such as cruisecritic.com are a good resource for checking out the local tour companies.

The biggest risk when taking independent excursions is - if you don't make it back to the ship in time, it **may** set sail without you. I've stood on the deck and watched people get left at the dock as they watched the ship sail away. (Most of the time this involved alcohol & losing track of time but that is another topic. That would go under free entertainment during your cruise!)

If you're planning an excursion that will take more than half of your day in port, I recommend booking through the cruise line. If the excursion that you booked through the cruise line runs past the ship's departure time, the ship will make every effort to make sure you are on back on board before it sets sail. If not, the cruise line is responsible for getting you to your next port. If you're **at all** nervous that you won't make it back and think it will ruin your day because you're worrying about it, then buy the peace of mind, pay a little extra and go with the ship excursions.

One more thing I would like to add is that venturing off on your own to hang out with locals and see how the locals live is not always a good idea. There are certain ports I personally would not feel safe wandering off on my own and exploring. Two of them that immediately come to mind would be Jamaica and Belize.

We tried this once in Jamaica and as we started walking, a

local came up trying to lead us off the main road. A polite, "no thank you" did not faze him. In fact, three more of his friends came up and started walking with us (in other words surrounding us), trying to get us to go off into an alley. We quickly realized venturing off was not a good idea and turned back – as quickly as possible. We ended up booking a ship excursion that day and had a great time.

If you plan on getting off the ship, take the part of your daily bulletin that gives you the contact information for emergencies when on shore. This will help you in the event you don't make it back on board and the ship leaves without you.

Chapter 9. Ports of Call

There are so many ports of call in the Bahamas, Caribbean, specialty cruises such as the Panama Canal, Alaska, Hawaii, it would be a very long book to cover each port. Living in Florida has given me lots of opportunities to visit the Bahamas and Caribbean ports numerous times over the years so I'll try to give you a feel for some of those ports and islands.

Before you get off the ship in port, make sure you have your sail and sign card, passport (or birth certificate and photo ID), cash, credit card, port contact information that can be found in your daily newsletter and a watch so you can make sure you stay on ship's time and make it back before the ship departs.

Almost all the islands offer similar excursions: snorkeling, a day at the beach, sightseeing tours, bike tours, shopping trips, horseback riding, kayaking, etc. I'll try to point out specific items in each of the below ports that make it unique.

If you shop for trinkets in the Caribbean or Bahamas ports, bartering with the vendors is expected. Don't automatically pay the original asking price. Chances are, they will sell it cheaper than originally offered or give you a discount if you buy more than one item.

Grand Cayman Island

One thing to mention about the ports. The majority of the time, the ships are able to dock right at the port. There are a few such as Grand Cayman and Belize that have tender ships that take you to shore. There is no charge for taking the ship's tenders.

Nassau, Bahamas. This is one of the busiest ports for cruise ships and there are always several ships there. The Straw Market and some unique restaurants including Senor Frog is within walking distance of the ship.

Atlantis Hotel, Paradise Island is a beautiful resort. You can buy day passes to the water park at this resort. I've been here quite a few times but never purchased the water park pass. Most people say it is worth every penny but I think during peak seasons when a lot of other ships are in port at the same time, the water park gets very congested and I hear more complaints that it was overcrowded and not worth the cost.

Atlantis Resort – Paradise Island, Bahamas

Freeport, Bahamas. There's not much to do right at the port. They've added a couple of popular bar/restaurants very close by but for anything else, you'll need to take a bus/shuttle to the other side of the island to get to the beach or decent shops. This would be a good port to book an excursion. If not, you can grab a taxi and head to the beach on your own.

St. Thomas. St. Thomas is famous for its beautiful beaches and great deals on jewelry. Magens Bay is rated one of the most beautiful beaches in the world and is definitely worth a visit. I've gotten some really good deals on diamond and gold jewelry here. Even if you don't plan on buying something, the shops are right at the port and fun to look around if you have some time to kill.

You're also walking distance to the Sky Lift. The lift takes you to the top of a steep hill that has a nice bar/restaurant area and panoramic views of the bay and cruise ships. (The first picture in my book is taken from the top.) It is "at your leisure" so you can spend as much time as you want once you get there.

St. Martin/St. Maarten. This island is part French and part Dutch *and* my personal favorite. A tour around the island to see the difference between the two countries is very interesting. Want to watch a plane land just above your head? Make sure you visit Maho Beach. If you want to drop a few coins and try your luck in one of the casinos, be sure to stop at Philipsburg's Front Street. There's a ferry boat at the docked port and for a small fee, they will shuttle you back and forth between Philipsburg and your ship.

Our last stop in St. Maarten last year was a little disappointing. There were more ships in this port than I have ever seen! I counted eight ships that day including, Royal Caribbean's Allure of the Seas – one of the largest passenger ships currently sailing. Good grief!! There were tons of people everywhere. It's still my favorite port but that definitely put a damper on the excitement!

TIP! To find out what (and how many) other cruise ships will be in a specific port on a certain day, check out ports.cruisett.com.

San Juan, Puerto Rico. Fort San Felipe del Morro is a short walk from the port and if you like history, this is worth a visit. You can walk the grounds for free but will have to pay to enter the fort. Old San Juan is a short walk from the ship, as well, and has some interesting shops. This is not my favorite island. I've been there several times, including at night and there have been a few times I haven't felt entirely safety. The streets are narrow with lots of little alleys and sometimes got the feeling I was being watched.

Castillo de San Felipe del Morro – San Juan, Puerto Rico

Belize. The cruise ship doesn't dock in Belize. You'll have to take a tender boat to shore. Belize has an amazing barrier reef with some of the best ocean life you will ever see. We once took a snorkeling excursion to the reef. The excursion was booked through the cruise line and they picked us up right from the ship (in other words, we did not have to go ashore and then turn around and take the excursion boat back out.)

On another visit, we did the Cave Tubing excursion and that was a lot of fun. This one may not be for everyone since it involves a lot of walking and uphill climbs while carrying your inner tube.

The cruise ship tender boats drop you off in a small shopping area near Belize City. There's not much to do and last time we were there, this area was fenced off so locals can't get into the tourist area. The gates are manned by armed guards. Personally, I would not wander past those guarded gates on my own.

Costa Maya. This port is not as developed as some of the others. At least is wasn't last time we were there – and it's been a few years. It has a very nice area right where the ship docks with pools and swim up bars, live music and restaurants along with shops to keep you entertained for an afternoon.

On one visit to Costa Maya we visited the Mayan Ruins of

Chacchoben. If you're interested in history and Mayan culture, I highly recommend this tour. Take sturdy shoes and bug repellant with you.

Grand Turk. This is another small island that docks and has a nice beach area and other amenities only a short walk from the ship. Jimmy Buffett's Margaritaville is nearby and very popular with cruise ship passengers. There's a large pool area – not too deep – and a swim up bar that looked pretty cool.

There's a FlowRider right next to Margaritaville, similar to the one on Royal Caribbean's newer ships. It's about $30 for an hour (both children and adults).

Grand Turk – Turks and Caicos. Free Beach Chairs/Snorkeling (Yep, that's me!)

The last time we were there, we hauled our snorkel gear ashore. At the end of the dock, head to the beach on the left hand side (closer to Margaritaville). I didn't snorkel but my husband did and he said you don't have to go too far out to see a wide variety of tropical fish.

The lounge chairs are free to use but some of them were in kinda rough shape this last visit. If you're the only ship in port, it'll be easy to find a good seat. If there's another ship there the same day, it's a little harder to find a shady spot to hang out. The beach to the right is just as nice and tends to be a little less crowded. (People seem to gravitate towards the action at Margaritaville which is to the left).

There are some smaller beach bars a bit of a walk down from the ship but prices aren't any cheaper than what you're going to pay at Margaritaville. We tried to get WiFi right off the ship and it was nearly impossible. We finally gave up and walked down to Jack's Shack, ordered a drink and they gave us the code to access WiFi which worked pretty good.

You might want to leave someone behind to watch your stuff if you plan on taking a dip in the ocean. There was a guy not far from us complaining that someone stole his sandals off one of the chairs.

Mexico. We've been to Mexico a bunch of times. It's one of the larger ports with so many different excursions available. The cruise ships dock in Cozumel. We've done everything from clear kayaking, to snorkeling to visiting the Mayan Ruins in Tulum in this port. All are worthwhile excursions. My personal favorite of all time – out of any cruise - going anywhere. Drum roll please.........the Mayan Ruins! (A very, very close second is The Money Bar.)

As far as the Tulum ruins excursion, I highly recommend booking through the cruise line. It will take almost your entire time in port: first a boat ride, then a walk through Playa del Carmen to shuttle buses and then a looong ride to the ruins followed by another walk to the ruins themselves. If you're interested in Mayan ruins or history, this is a worthwhile excursion. The scenery is breathtaking and our tour guide was worth every penny. After the tour we had some free time to wander the shops or eat lunch. Taking the recommendation from our awesome guide, we had a delicious lunch of fish tacos and sampled their local beer.

Tulum Mayan Ruins – Quintana Roo, Mexico

Cliff Overlooking Ocean - Tulum Ruins, Mexico

My second favorite was on one of our most recent cruises. We discovered a great place to go snorkeling for the cost of a $10 cab ride (one way - for all four of us). So for $20 (remember, I bring my own snorkel gear), all four of us had a chance to snorkel. Way cheaper than the price of even one snorkeling excursion booked through the cruise line.

If one of your port stops is Cozumel and you are on a tight budget, do yourself a favor and check out the Money Bar Beach Club (Carretera Costera Sur Km. 6, Zona Hotelera, 77600 Cozumel, Quitana Roo, Mexico.) Sounds like a long, confusing address, but all you need to tell the cab driver is to take you to the Money Bar. Don't believe me? Check out the reviews on Tripadvisor!

If you get there early enough, you can grab some nice lounge chairs or a table with a festive tropical umbrella to keep you from melting in the heat. There is not a bad seat in the house. The bathrooms are clean and you can rent a locker to store your belongings.

From any spot, you'll have the most magnificent view of the Gulf. The waiters will start coming around later in the morning to see if you'd like to try a fruity, tropical drink or take a look at the menu. As a courtesy for using their chairs and umbrellas, they encourage you to order something. There are steps leading right into the crystal clear water where just a short swim will lead you to a variety of beautiful tropical fish swimming around right below you.

All 3 Pictures are of the Money Bar Beach Club, Cozumel, Mexico

While we were there, several snorkeling boats arrived with visitors who paid **way** more than $10 to do the exact same thing!

When you're ready to head back to the ship, you shouldn't have any trouble finding a taxi to take you back. Just make your way to the Money Bar entrance and look across the street. Taxis park at the hotel, waiting to take tourists back to the port.

Private Islands. Most, if not all, cruise lines have their own private islands. If you're lucky enough to take a cruise and the itinerary includes a stop, make sure you go ashore! The private islands are for the exclusive use of their respective cruise lines and it can be a really wonderful vacation day. The islands are mostly unspoiled. Disney is the only line that docks right at the island. The rest rely on shuttles to ferry passengers to and from the island.

With shuttles, there's always a chance that the seas are too rough or the weather prohibits visiting the island. We missed visiting Half Moon Cay once due to rough seas. It was disappointing as our kids were with us on this cruise and really looking forward to this stop.

The shuttle typically takes 30 minutes or less to get to shore. On shore, there are only a handful of gift shops, bar areas, a large outdoor bbq pavilion the cruise line sets up for lunch on shore, restrooms, live music, inflatable water toys for the kids, nice lounge chairs, trails for walking, etc.

Coco Cay- Private Island, Royal Caribbean

Coco Cay – Private Island, Royal Caribbean.
Returning Tender Boat

One of the best perks of the private island ports is almost everything is free for that day: shuttle to shore, lunch on shore, lounge chairs (not including shell chairs) and hiking trails.

Extras would include alcoholic drinks, excursions (if offered) such as horseback riding, beach massages, renting out the cabanas (if offered) and anything purchased in the little shops. Most cruise lines charge to use the water inflatables, as well.

The beaches are pristine, there is no one following you around begging you to buy souvenirs and it's not crowded since you are the only ones on the island.

Cayman Islands. Grand Cayman. This is a tender port as the ship does not dock here. It's a very nice island and known for awesome scuba diving, a whole lot of banks, a turtle farm and - for being expensive. We found out the hard way that the price you see is not the price you pay! A nice, cool beverage at a local bar could be priced at $6 – but that $6 is Grand Cayman currency and is $7.32 in American dollars. (Current – 2014 exchange rate is $1 Cayman $1.22 USD)   On top of that, prices on this island are just plain higher than some of the others.

Downtown Grand Cayman – Cayman Islands

Chapter 10. Buying Beverages on Board

Tip #1. Maybe I should've put this at the very front of this book? Well, better late than never. If a cruise ship employee asks to see your card – you're probably = more-than-likely - going to be charged for something. When you board, you will see a lot of servers walking around with trays of exotic tropical drinks that are oh-so-tempting. Keep in mind you will be charged for these beverages. There are a few out there that do include a complimentary champagne or other beverage when you board but the majority of the larger lines (Royal Caribbean, Carnival, Norwegian, etc.) do not.

Some cruise lines have an allotted amount of beverages you

can bring on board. For example, Carnival allows a bottle of wine per person brought onboard in your carry-on. (Don't forget the wine opener.) Unopened sodas and water can also be brought on board certain cruise ships in limited quantities.

Royal Caribbean also allows one bottle of wine per person but last I checked, you had to put it in your checked bag. I always recommend bringing bottled water to consume in your cabin. The faucet water in the bathroom is not the best and I won't drink it. Yes, you can go to the Lido deck and grab a glass of water to take to your cabin but if you forget, it can be a long trip back to Lido just to get a drink. Or – skip all that and bring a filtered water bottle. Save money and space!

Most, if not all, cruise lines offer unlimited beverage cards to purchase. These can be bought on the first day and used the entire length of your cruise. A designated drink glass is normally provided and this is what you use to refill your (soda) beverages. They can be pricey so only you can decide if you'll drink enough sodas that'll make it worth it. Certain lines only offer certain brands, as well. If you love Coke and hate Pepsi but find out they only serve Pepsi products on your ship, if might be worth it to bring your own with you.

Unlimited Beverage Package – Royal Caribbean

MONEY SAVING TIP. If you plan on buying a beverage package or unlimited soda package, wait until the cruise ship is in international waters and you won't pay sales tax!

Many cruise lines now offer alcoholic beverage packages as well. Some lines make all guests in a cabin buy the packages (so you don't share) while others will let just one person purchase it.

Many others offer alcoholic drink specials at different times on different days. 2-for-1, a dollar off drink specials, happy hour drink specials, etc. Check your daily news bulletin to find out where and when.

Beverages included in the cost of the cruise are typically tea, orange juice or some kind of fruit juice, water and coffee. Espresso, Cappuccinos, alcoholic drinks and beverages at the specialty coffee counter and in the dining room are almost always extra.

Chapter 11. Dining, Dining & More Dining!

If you've heard anything about cruises, you already know that you can eat – a lot! One of the best things about cruising is all the choices. There's the breakfast buffet, the open seating for breakfast in the dining room, lunch in the dining room or café, the Lido Deck for burgers and hot dogs, room service, 24 Hour Pizza, the Pasta Bar, the Deli, Specialty Restaurants. Need I go on?   A recent cruise on Carnival Dream had the most options I have seen so far and included all the above plus a tasting bar, Burrito Bar, Tandoor, Mongolian Wok, Comedy Brunch, Chef's Steakhouse. I'm trying to remember them all but I might be missing a couple! If a Carnival cruise is in your future and you want to check out their current menus, a good site to visit is http://www.zydecocruiser.net/menus/CarnivalCruiseLineMenus.ht m

French Onion Soup

Prime Rib

Chocolate Chip Cookie w/Vanilla Ice Cream

The good news is – almost all the food is included, except for those Specialty Restaurants or ordering decadent pastries or other goodies at the coffee bar. I know some cruisers who book specialty restaurants every night while others have never stepped foot in one. We reserve those Specialty Restaurants for special occasions. And we've had some wonderful dinners there while others have been . . . not so great. Specialty restaurants are not "all you can eat" but servings are large and you won't leave hungry.

We like eating in the dining room. It is a chance to spiff up a bit and sample new dishes. There are normally 3 -4 appetizers, a couple salads, several main course offerings and a variety of desserts. The cruise lines do try hard to please everyone! There is almost always a fish or seafood, vegetarian dish, red meat and white meat option and a couple extras - just for good measure. Are there two appetizers that look interesting? Order both! There is no limit on what you can order so try something new and if you don't like it, get something else!

Smoked Turkey with Apples, Grapes & Walnuts
(Appetizer) Celebrity

There is a dress code for eating in the dining room. Check before you head down. I have actually seen them turn guests away who didn't meet the dress code standards.

Most cruise lines offer a couple different options for dining room schedule. Traditional seating and dining at your leisure. For the traditional seating, you are assigned the same dining time each evening and are seated at the same table. Typically, early dining is around 6:00 p.m. and late dining around 8:30 p.m. The other option, anytime dining, is a timeframe of around 6 p.m. – 9 p.m. Check the individual cruise line for specific times.

Norwegian Cruise Line is known for their "Freestyle Cruising" and there is no traditional seating at all.

With the traditional dining arrangements, if there are only two of you or sometimes even four people, they may seat you with a larger group of people. Some people enjoy meeting new people while others do not. So what happens if you're seated with a large group and you don't like it? Speak to the Maître d' after your first dinner and ask to be moved. They make every effort to accommodate and you will more than likely be moved to another table.

My Fair Lady Dining Room –
Enchantment of the Seas. RCCL

For anytime dining or the non-scheduled dining time, you can request a table for two. The cruise lines tend to squeeze those tables close together - but you don't have to start a conversation with the diners at the tables around you – unless, of course, you want to!

Things to consider before choosing what time to dine or your dining option is what ports you will be in during your cruise and what you plan to do on those days. If you have a lot of excursions booked and they will be running late in the day for each port, early dining might not work for you. If you have younger children and typically eat an early dinner at home, then late dining might not be the best choice for you.

Last but not least, especially if you are dining with a larger group, please show up for dinner on time. That will ensure others who are already at the table don't have to wait on you and, trust me, the waiters will appreciate staying on schedule. Rumor has it that at least one of the larger cruise lines will be implementing a new policy that if you have assigned dining time and show up after a set time – say you are 15 minutes late – you'll be turned away.

Breakfast – Main Dining Room. Celebrity

I have just a brief comment on room service. I've been on enough cruises to know this is a weak spot for all of them. No matter when you call to order, it seems you are on hold for EVER & it takes a very long time to have your food delivered. Regardless of how your experience goes, don't forget to tip the person who brings your order. It's not their fault if service is lacking - and they work very hard for those tips. Most cruise lines have added a nominal charge for ordering LATE NIGHT room service. This charge will be added to your onboard account. But you're still expected to tip!

Chapter 12. Tipping

Tipping should be factored in when determining how much you plan on spending on your cruise. The majority of what the crew earns on the ship is what you give them in tips. The average charge should be around $12 - $15 per day per person (your cruise line will give you direction on what amount is appropriate). This covers your room stewards, all service in the dining room and café. Suite guests will be charged a higher per-day rate but they have more services available to them.

When you order a beverage on board – alcoholic or otherwise, an automatic gratuity will be added. Same thing with the Spa. An automatic gratuity is added. There is a line on the receipt where you can add an extra tip if you want.

The above per day tips do not cover baggage handlers, butlers/valets (if you're lucky enough to be in one of those fancy suites) and room service.

Chapter 13. Travel Insurance

Here's my disclaimer. I've never actually purchased the travel insurance. I live in Florida and within a few hours' drive of every single Florida port. Our children are all grown so therefore, travel insurance isn't important – to me/us. At least until the grandkids come!

If you got a last minute, cheap cruise and don't have to worry about distance to the cruise port, potential family emergencies or other circumstances that might come into play and force you to miss your cruise, then purchasing travel insurance might not be necessary.

If you spent a small fortune and are flying to port or driving a long distance, you should consider travel insurance. Anything can happen and it would be terrible to miss your cruise and be out all that money.

I would check both the cruise line's insurance and independent insurance to find out exactly what the insurance covers. From what I understand, the coverage can vary – a lot.

Along with that, I recommend arriving a day early. This will give you time to relax and not stress that you are going to miss the cruise, especially in the winter months.

If you're flying home after your cruise, I recommend flying out at least 6 hours after you are scheduled to arrive back in port. A lot of things can happen. Customs can hold all passengers on the ship (happened to me), the ship may have mechanical issues making it late into port (happened to me) or weather can be a factor (also happened to me). Don't spend a week relaxing only to get stressed out about catching your flight home.

A little off topic now - but those shuttles that the cruise line offers and costs lots of money? Don't do it. A taxi will almost always be cheaper and get you to and from the airport a whole lot faster. There are tons of them parked outside the port when you leave. If there's room and you can find another passenger to share the cost of the taxi, you can save even more money.

Chapter 14. Staying Safe Onboard

I wasn't even sure about adding this topic since you use the same common sense on a cruise ship that you would traveling anywhere else but they do have a couple special exceptions on cruise ships that are worth mentioning.

Sail & Sign/onboard room card. As I said before, this card is given to you when you first board the ship and it has everything on it. Treat it like gold. Or money. Because it is! It is used as your room key, it is used for any onboard purchases, you need it when getting on and off the ship in port - it even tells the crew your status as a cruiser.

You'll need to keep this card with you at all times both on ship and when you visit various ports. When you leave the ship at port, it lets the crew know that you've left and checks you back in when you return. The greatest safety feature of this card is the only thing it shows is your name and Folio or account number. It does not give your cabin number or any other info.

Here's the bad part of carrying this card that has everything on it. If you lose it and someone finds your card, they can take it anywhere on the ship and charge stuff to your account. Since you don't carry photo id around with you, no one ever checks to make sure you and your card belong together. Someone could run up a hefty tab on your account if they had it long enough. If you lose your card, go immediately to the guest services desk and have that card cancelled and a new card issued.

There are in-room safes in almost all cabins. I suggest leaving all your valuables in there. I have never (never say never) had an issue with room stewards or been worried they might take something, but the room stewards will sometimes leave cabin doors open when they're cleaning more than one room at a time. Call me paranoid, but I think it would be fairly easy for someone to sneak in your room and grab something off the counter (like a phone or a piece of jewelry). You'll need a card or pin number to set your in-room safe. If the safe requires a card, I don't recommend using your actual credit card (then you wouldn't be able to lock it in the safe.) Other cards will work. The last card we used was our Panera Bread point's card.

If you have a cabin with a balcony, keep your balcony door shut and locked when you're not in there. It would be pretty easy for your neighbor to climb around or over the divider and enter your room. Yes, you would think no one would be stupid enough to try it but I watched some teenage boys do it one time.

On the last day of your cruise, you'll have to decide if you're going to take your luggage with you when you leave the ship in the morning or if you plan on letting the crew pick up your luggage to be off-loaded and placed in the designated pick up area. If you decide to let them take your luggage, you'll be able to exit the ship a little later in the morning. If you chose self-disembarkation, the benefit is you will be one of the first passengers off in the morning. Which means you'll have to get up pretty early. We've been off the ship and in our car before 8:00 in the morning before. Just make sure you are able to handle carrying all your luggage off and possibly navigating escalators or stairs with all that luggage.

If you decide to pick up your luggage after getting off the ship, you'll be given luggage tags the night before. Typically, the room steward will leave them in your room. If not, you can pick some up at guest services. Make sure your old tags are off before putting the new ones on. Make sure these bags are sitting outside your cabin before the designated deadline the night before. The time varies by cruise line. Sometimes it is 11 p.m., sometimes midnight.

If you do set your luggage out, make sure there is nothing of value inside! Also, make sure you keep a change of clothing and any needed toiletries with you for the last morning. You can also lock that luggage if you want (and I recommend).

Chapter 15. Staying in Touch With Reality

Internet. If you can't leave the world completely behind, you can purchase internet minutes and use your own computer or the computers provided in the internet café. The more minutes you buy, the more you'll save. If you think you will be using the computer a lot, buy more minutes up front. The ship's computers are not nearly as fast as the one at home. A quick check of email will take twice as long! They also run specials on internet minutes such as days you are in port or the first day you get on so check the daily bulletins.

TIP: Log on, download your emails, log off and type all your replies. Log back on and hit send. This will save you some valuable minutes.

A lot of the ports have internet cafes where you can buy internet minutes for a fraction of the price the ship charges & it's a lot faster. I found if you ask any of the crew onboard the ship, the best place to find internet in port, they'll be happy to tell you!

Phone. All cruise ships operate with a service called "Cellular at Sea." The cell phone "tower" is on board the ship and links to the cell phone grid via satellite. The charges for using your cell phone onboard will be very high so check with guest services for current rates. This charge will be in addition to what your cell phone provider charges.

It will be a little cheaper to use your cell phone to check in once you get off the ship and use land based cell service while in port. Check with your cell phone provider before you leave to find out what you need to do to use your cell phone while away and what those charges will be.

Chapter 16. Life Onboard. What Not to Miss

This is more geared towards first time cruisers but even if you've cruised before, you might learn something new.

Mandatory Safety Drill. I hear stories all the time about people who hide out to avoid this safety drill. In light of the Costa Concordia disaster, Carnival Triumph's engine failure and Royal Caribbean's recent fire, this highlights the importance of attending the safety drill. Hopefully you will never need it, but keep in mind it only takes a short amount of time out of your vacation and could save your life.

I once heard a couple who took a back-to-back cruise. They attended the mandatory safety drill for the first cruise but hid out and skipped the second one and they were removed from the ship before they could begin their second cruise!

Boleros Lounge – Royal Caribbean

Entertainment. There are tons of things you can do onboard. From Las Vegas style shows to belly flop contest to spa treatments (upcharge) to ice carvings to comedy clubs to dance classes, there is something for everyone. Make sure you read the daily schedule of events the room steward leaves in your room each evening for the following day. It has great information and lists every event that's going on during the day.

A tip for the evening shows, go early! The best seats fill up quickly so try to get there at least half an hour before the show starts to get a decent seat.

On Royal Caribbean, book as many of the shows allowed as soon as you possibly can. The first time we sailed Royal Caribbean, we didn't realize we needed to make advance reservations for the ice show. When we got onboard and tried to make a reservation, we were basically "waitlisted." We had to wait until all the people with reservations were inside the theater and then we got the seats that were left - and they weren't great seats. If you'll be cruising on one of RCCL's mega ships like Allure or Oasis of the Seas, you can reserve several of the shows in advance and I highly recommend this.

Live Music in the Centrum

Relaxing by the Pool. Admittedly, I don't do this very often. I think the pools are too small, crowded and most are saltwater, which I don't care for. Since I live in Florida, we have a pool and lots of warm weather and sunshine, I just don't feel the need to hang out there.

The lido deck and pool area are fun for people watching, they have lots of great music and activities to watch and participate in. And if you're coming from up North, especially in the winter time, the sunshine is wonderful!

One word of caution. You can get a sunburn very quickly in the Caribbean or Bahamas. I see it every cruise. The first day, there are lots and lots of people laying out all afternoon. The next day you see them they have a bad sunburn. It's so easy to burn and hard to tell that you're burned until it's too late. Use lots of sunscreen and apply often.

Pool Deck

Casino. Most cruise ships have casinos on board. There are no casinos on Disney cruise ships, though. They also do not have casinos on sailings in Hawaii.   If you leave from California and cruise to Hawaii, the casinos will be open for part of the trip. Although once they get within a certain radius of the Hawaiian Islands, they will close the casino down. They're not very big but normally have a variety of slot machines from a penny on up. They also have table games including Roulette, Craps and Blackjack.

Most of the lines offer classes that teach you how to play the table games and have discounts at certain times of the day.

Most casinos allow smoking but also offer a non-smoking area, although this doesn't help too much as the casinos are small and the smoke permeates into the non-smoking area.

Several lines have slot tournaments for the duration of the cruise. There is a one-time fee to buy in and if you're lucky, you can win a nice chunk of change.

Casino

Shopping. Some items you purchase on board or in the various ports are tax free, up to a certain amount. This includes cigarettes, alcohol and jewelry. That in itself can save you quite a bit of amount of money.

Alcohol can be a bargain but keep in mind, if you buy it during the cruise, you cannot take it back to your cabin. When you get back on board the ship after a day in port, the crew will take the alcohol from you and then either deliver it to your cabin the last evening of your cruise or have a designated pick up location. Same thing if you buy it in one of their shops. They hold it until the end of the cruise. Why you ask? Money. If you bought – or brought – your own alcohol on board, then they couldn't sell you their super-expensive drinks!

The stores will sell clearance items but I found they wait until the very end of the cruise to get rid of some merchandise. By all means, if you find something you want to buy – get it – but maybe wait until the last day to see if it goes on sale!

Children's Programs. If you have children, cruise lines have programs tailored to every age group. They have activities ranging from science experiments to scavenger hunts and art activities to pajama parties. There are activities from the very young on up to older teens. The first day you embark, check the activity schedule for sign-up locations and times with the activity coordinators.

Circle C Club (12 – 14 Years Old) – Carnival Dream

Art Auction. I've heard numerous complaints regarding the art auctions on cruise ships. I've been to a few but never purchased. To me, the art looks like print copies that are not worth what people pay. It's an easy way to be entertained and most throw in free champagne during the auction. If you're interested in art and checking out the auction on board, Google "cruise ship art auctions" so you are aware of what passenger complaints have been.

Bingo. Everybody loves Bingo, right? Bingo can be fun and from what I have seen, it's very popular! You can buy Bingo cards using your onboard credit account. Some of the jackpots are sizeable and most cruise lines even have a grand prize with a chance to win a cruise!

Spa and Fitness Center. I've never purchased a Spa treatment but use the fitness center regularly. They're usually not very large but offer a nice variety of exercise equipment and weights. Most cruise lines also offer classes for a fee, as well. Some cruise lines offer discounts or specials at the spa on port days when they aren't as busy.

Adults Only Solarium – Enchantment of the Seas

Behind the Scenes Tour. We've done the Behind the Scenes Tour. If you're curious about how a cruise ship really runs, this is a not-to-be-missed tour! It can be a little pricey but you definitely get a glimpse of what it really takes to keep the ship sailing smoothly. Ours took us on a tour of the engine room, backstage dressing room for the dancers, a glimpse of the laundry room, the galley and storage areas for all that food and even a tour of the crew area and their dining room. Our tour ended in the bridge where we met the Captain. It's amazing how much food, how much laundry and the sheer power – and people - it takes to keep those enormous ships afloat and moving. Just a warning, closed-toed shoes are required for the tour. You cannot do the tour with sandals or flip-flops!

Active Activities. You're tired of sitting in a lounge chair and you want to DO something. Well, if you're on a Royal Caribbean cruise, you might just be in luck. Some of their ships offer rock wall climbing, ice skating, zip lining or boxing. Some even have a FlowRider.

If you're on Norwegian, you might be able to try out their bowling alley. Most cruise lines offer ping pong or a basketball court. Many have mini golf. If staying active is very important to you or you have children with LOTS of energy, be sure to find out what activities your cruise has to offer.

Debarkation Talk. This has to do with getting off the ship at the end of the cruise and what you need to do. Customs is strict about filling out the correct paperwork/form and it can be confusing so if this is your first cruise, go to the debarkation talk. It could save you some serious headaches. If, by chance, you miss the talk, they will show it on the television in your cabin.

My own personal preference is self-assist. My husband and I try to pack light enough so that we can carry (or drag) our luggage off the ship ourselves. One thing to keep in mind is that you may not be able to find an available elevator that lets you off where you need to exit so you'll need to be able to safely carry your luggage up or down the stairs to the exit. If you can do this, you will be one of the first in line to leave.

If you would rather leave your luggage outside the night before, sleep in a bit later that last morning and have a leisurely breakfast, make sure your luggage is locked and outside your cabin before the deadline the night before. We never, ever leave anything of value in these suitcases. You'll want to keep a change of clothes, any medication, all valuables, your passports/visa/birth certificate and ID with you. You will also need your sail and sign card to get off the ship.

Bon Voyage!

I personally believe that a cruise vacation is the best vacation "under the sun"! My tips are things I wish I had known before sailing on my first cruise. I hope the tips and advice I've given you here will help to make your upcoming cruise the best vacation you can imagine! So...Get Ready, Set, Cruise!

If you've enjoyed this book, please take a moment to post a positive review on Amazon. I would really appreciate it.

Thank you!

Don't Forget To Check Out My Other Travel Books!

Florida Beaches: A Guide to the Best Beaches in Central Florida

Fun Things To Do In Orlando, Florida – Insider's Guide to Orlando Attractions and More